...hy Asiedu

The ABC of E-Business

Timothy Asiedu

The ABC of E-Business

Scholars' Press

Imprint

Any brand names and product names mentioned in this book are subject to trademark, brand or patent protection and are trademarks or registered trademarks of their respective holders. The use of brand names, product names, common names, trade names, product descriptions etc. even without a particular marking in this work is in no way to be construed to mean that such names may be regarded as unrestricted in respect of trademark and brand protection legislation and could thus be used by anyone.

Cover image: www.ingimage.com

Publisher:
Scholars' Press
is a trademark of
International Book Market Service Ltd., member of OmniScriptum Publishing Group
17 Meldrum Street, Beau Bassin 71504, Mauritius

ISBN: 978-613-8-94809-4

THE ABC

OF

e-BUSINESS

Timothy K. Asiedu

Table of Contents

INTRODUCTION

E-Business helps to run our businesses faster through electronic means or using the Internet. E-Business improves running your businesses in an economical way, but the watchword will be putting good strategies in place for the organization. The Internet and other technologies are helping a lot in growing our organizations and other businesses. It all starts with having a good list of customers and using the right technologies like website and others. The book has been made practical and also easy to follow like ABC. In going through the materials in the book, you will encounter many issues you face in the business environment.

The book is recommended for everyone in the business environment, especially Chief Executive Officers, Managers, Supervisors and IT Professionals. The book has a lot of examples to make the study of e-Business and e-Commerce as easy as possible. Most of the materials treated in this book were issues encountered at the workplaces of the author and also during his research studies. Based on the experiences in Information Technology and Business Management of the author, the material in the book has been presented in a way to make e-Business and e-Commerce interesting.

Chapter one focuses on common terms you will encounter in the electronic business environments. You certainly need a full understanding of these keywords or terms to appreciate your understanding of the discipline electronic business and electronic commerce.

Chapter Two tackles the strategies required for our e-business initiative. Certainly you can have the best technologies and business models for your e-business initiative, but without good strategies put in place for your e-business environments you are bound to fail.

Chapter Three touches on the Benefits and Success of e-business for our business environment. This is a must read chapter since it helps a lot to clarify the benefits and success associated with our e-business initiative.

Chapter Four talks about the Customer, an invaluable stakeholder of the organization. Without customers there is no business. So in order not to waste your time in building a good e-business initiative with profitable customers, it is important to start your initiative by aligning yourself with list of good customers. Good customers will help your business to be profitable.

Chapter Five dwells on the Security of our e-Business environments. Without good Information Security strategies, our business environment is bound to have a problem with our Business Continuity. It is quite important to develop good Information Security for your business environment in order for not security threats and others to thwart your effort in running your e-business initiative.

Chapter Six focuses on the IPv6, an invaluable Protocol for the e-Business. IPv6, an aspect of TCP/IP is the new protocol for developing of our Internet infrastructure after IPv4, the old protocol. Certainly, this new protocol, IPv6 is very important for the growth of the Internet, which the old protocol IPv4 was co-developed by Dr. Vinton Cerf in the mid 1970.

Chapter Seven dwells on - Technology, a Platform to market your Organization. Through this chapter, common Social Media platforms like Facebook, Twitter, LinkedIn, YouTube and others which help to grow our businesses will be familiarized by the readers of the book. Other Business Management principles which help in digital marketing are also discussed in this chapter.

Chapter Eight titled, "The Internet, an Invaluable Resource" touches on the Internet and its capability for the business environment. The Internet is a key resource for the e-Business initiative and its services have changed the way we do business globally.

DEDICATION

To my Father: Daniel Anka Asiedu, the wisest man I knew

To my Mother: Emily Osam Forson, the most caring woman I knew

To my Wife: Esther, the most loving woman I know

To my two daughters: Andrea & Christabel, the smartest girls I have come across.

Chapter One

Key Words in eBusiness

Network

Network is a system which involves information transfer. Computer network include all hardware and software required to connect with other electronic devices to a channel so that they can communicate with each other. Devices that communicate with other devices on the network are called nodes, stations or simply network devices.

There are three (3) main types of networks, which are LAN (i.e. Local Area Networks), MAN (i.e. Metropolitan Area Network) and WAN (i.e. Wide Area Network). Normally the LAN, MAN and WAN are differentiated by the geographical area and the speed of communication of the networks.

LAN

The Local Area Network (i.e. LAN) is normally used to connect computers which are geographically close. For instance the computers in the office of TIM Technology Services Ltd (TTS) are connected together in a LAN.

Within TTS, we use TCP/IP as the protocol (or rather suits of protocols) which is used on LANs. Other protocols which can be used on LAN are Novell Netware or IPX, but they are not supported in our organization. Normally LAN technologies are used when speed is required. Unfortunately, LANs give this speed by limiting the distance the data can be sent over. A typical LAN speed is anything from 2Mbps to 2Gbps.

WAN

A Wide Area Network is normally used to connect computers which are geographically distant. For instance the Internet in our office at TIM Technology Services Ltd., Accra, Ghana connected by Vodafone Ghana Ltd uses WAN. Normally, WAN work at a slower speed than other network technologies such as LAN or MAN but over greater distances. A typically WAN will run at speeds of 9.6 kbps to 45 Mbps. Apart from TCP/IP there are new network protocols emerging such as frame relay which does away with much of the error checking as they assume that the underlying physical network is more error free. Nowadays, this is a valid assumption to make and allow greater efficiency as more data is sent instead of error checking.

Network Topologies

A network topology describes the physical layout of the network medium and attached devices. There are many type of network topologies we have, including the following:

1) Mesh
2) Star
3) Bus
4) Ring
5) Hybrid

LMS

LMS is the acronym for the Learning Management System specifically developed for managing online courses, distributing course materials and allowing collaboration between students and teachers.

Micro-Learning

Micro - Learning involves learning in smaller steps, and goes hand-in-hand with traditional e-Learning. Normally, activities of micro-learning are based on short term lessons, courses or project. In this manner, information is released to the student in smaller bits. In such a situation, instead of teaching the student at a go, the topic for the course is broken into smaller lesson plans or projects.

Protocols

Protocols are nothing but a set of strict rules for the exchange of information. A typical protocol is the TCP/IP (i.e. Transport Control Protocol / Internet Protocol). The US Defence Department, through its Defense Advanced Research Projects Agency (i.e. DARPA) funded a project to look into internet working. In the mid 1970s, the research began in earnest and was carried out by various US government agencies, educational and research bodies. The result of that research has produced the TCP/IP; two protocols TCP and IP.

Basic Data Communication Model

At the most fundamental level, networks are systems that permit communication of information. The basic components of any communication model are a sender, a receiver, a medium through which the information flows (often called a channel), and a message. The sender and receiver could be two people talking, or a PC and a mainframe computer, or a satellite and a reception dish. The medium could be a telephone line, a cable, or the air through which microwave travel.

Unbounded media

Unbounded media (sometimes called wireless media) host the transmission and reception of electromagnetic signals without a device that constrains the signals. The air is the best example of unbounded media. Microwave, infrared, laser links and radio are examples of transmissions using unbounded media.

internet

An internet (local case i) is a collection of networks joined by a common protocol (normally TCP/IP) to create a single logical network.

Internet

The Internet (uppercase I) is a worldwide collection of internets which grew out of the original ARPANET. The Internet uses TCP/IP to link many internets into one logical worldwide network. This means that you have the ability to connect to computers which are not actually part of your own organization. The Internet can be seen as a special network of networks.

TCP/IP

TCP/IP (Transmission Control Protocol / Internet Protocol) is an example of a packet switched network. The idea of packet switching was first introduced in the mid 1960's as was needed to transmit data (packets) across a network efficiently and reliably. Therefore, the US Defence Department, through its Defence Advanced Research Project Agency (DARPA) funded a project to look into internetworking. In the mid 1970's, the research began in earnest and was carried out by various US government agency, educational and research bodies. The result of this research has become known as the TCP/IP protocol suite or more commonly, TCP/IP after the two main protocols in the protocol suite.

TCP/IP

Features
In fact TCP/IP did not become popular because the protocols were "free", but the protocol has several important features which are as follows:

- Open "standards" as defined in the RFCs.

This means that TCP/IP is independent from any specific hardware and software.

- Physical Independence:

  TCP/IP is also independent from the underlying physical network. This gives the TCP/IP the ability to be used over virtually any type of physical network, such as X.25, Ethernet or UUCP.

- Common Addressing:

  TCP gives each host on a network a unique network address which has a standard format. This allows any network device to "talk" to a printer via TCP/IP.

- Application Standards:

  TCP/IP protocol is standardized for user services. Examples of such services are telnet/rlogin (remote login), ftp (file transfer) and smtp (electronic mail).

- Network Management:

  TCP/IP includes a particular protocol called Simple Network Management Protocol (SNMP) which normally allows both local and remote network management.

ARPANET

In 1980, the TCP/IP was sufficiently developed and standardised that it was deployed on a network called ARPANET. The ARPANET initially formed the backbone to which all other networks were connected, forming the first internetwork. Eventually the funding provided by the US Government started to disappear for the backbone, and the ARPANET became known as the Internet.

ADSL

The most common **broadband** type currently available in the Australian Market and some other parts of the world including Africa is **ADSL** (**Asymmetric Digital Subscriber Line**). This service enables high speed data transmission through existing telephone lines without interfering with normal telephone operations. The ADSL modem / router can operate as an ADSL, ADSL 2+, or Annex M modem that works with most ISPs. Zoom Telephonics lets you quickly set it up using any web-browser. Once connected, it comes with wireless security, DoS protection, firewall, and more to safeguard the network. If you already have a modem that was provided from the service provider, you can reconfigure one of the LAN ports as a WAN, enabling it as just a router. Additionally, the intuitive graphical user interface makes it easy to configure the ADSL modem/router as a bridge. ADSL Technology is the Internet technology provided by Vodafone Ghana Ltd. Vodafone Ghana provides ADSL Internet technology to TIM Technology Services Ltd., the organization founded by the author of this book.

Router

The router is Information Technology equipment which helps in distributing Wireless signal from the ISP to the end user equipment for Internet. The router used by the author of this paper is manufactured by Huawei Technologies Ltd. and was provided by Vodafone Ghana Ltd., a telecommunication organization which is the ISP of TIM Technology Services Ltd., Accra, Ghana. Internet is provided by Vodafone Ghana Ltd to TIM Technology Services Ltd through the Huawei router via the Vodafone Ghana telephone handset using ADSL technology. Once TIM Technology Services Ltd. (TTS) pays for its Internet services fee, and the router is powered; the entire office of TTS is provided with wireless signal for its IT equipment.

Information Security

Information Security is the security of the Information Systems on our PCs in the offices and others. Observing basic rules and others so that you can have your Computer systems running all the time is all about Information Security. Not only what has been mentioned is required but Information Security is also about the protection of your documents in the office.
.

Internet Fraud

Internet or the Electronic fraud is the piracy of Information for pecuniary benefits. Thus any act carried out with criminal deception using Information Technology as a medium is Electronic Fraud. So much money is lost through Electronic Fraud everyday, so it is important that we have very good Information Security systems in our offices.

Firewall

Firewall is a security system installed on a corporate network to check intruders or hackers from entering the network system. An example of the CISCO Firewall system is CISCO ASA 5500 – X.

Information Security Policy

Documented policies are normally put together in the office for use by all Computer Users. The local Information Security Policy must contain statement of management intention supporting the goals and principles of Information Security:

Internet Service Providers (ISP's)

The Internet Service Providers or the ISP's are responsible for distributing the IPv6 Internet Addresses to the end users. Each ISP receives the Internet Addresses from their respective Regional Internet Registries (i.e.RIR) mentioned below.

Regional Internet Registries (i.e. RIR)

The Regional Internet Registries are five (5) in number globally and are responsible for distributing the IP Address (currently using IPv6 Internet Protocol address, before that we were using IPv4 Internet Protocol address). Although IPv6 replaced IPv4, IPv4 is still in use on certain Network. The RIR distributes the Internet Address to various Internet Service Providers in the various countries. The five (5) RIR are as follows:

> ➤ AfriNIC: AfriNIC is the Internet Registry for Africa and it has the Url: www.afrinic.net. AfriNIC is responsible for the distribution of Internet Address (thus: IPv6) to the various Internet Service Providers (i.e. ISPs) in Africa.
> ➤ APNIC: APNIC is the Internet Registry for Asia Pacific region. It has the URL: www. apnic.net. So APNIC is responsible for distributing the IP Address in that region.
> ➤ ARIN: ARIN is the Internet Registry for Canada, many Caribbean and the North Atlantic islands, and the United States. It has the URL: www.arin.net. ARIN is responsible for distributing the IP Address in that region.
> ➤ LACNIC: LACNIC is the Internet Registry for Latin America and the Carribean. It has the URL: www.lacnic.net LACNIC is responsible for distributing the Internet Address in that region.
> ➤ RIPE NCC: RIPE NIC is the Internet registry for Europe, the Middle East and parts of Central Asia. It has the URL: www.ripe.net. RIPE NCC is responsible for distributing the IP Addresses to the Internet Service Providers in that region.

E-Learning

E-Learning, incuding Massive Open Online Courses (i.e. MOCC.org): MOOC with the acronym Massive Open Online Courses is an online course aimed at unlimited participants and open access through the World Wide Web (i.e. WWW) of the Internet. MOOC is widely researched in the development of distance education and emerged as popular form of learning in 2012. MOOC is a free online course available for anyone to enrol. MOOCs which can be accessed at URL: www.mooc.org is an extension of edx with URL: www.edx.org, a leader in online courses. MOOCs provide an affordable program, which is flexible in learning new skills. You can advance your career and deliver quality educational experiences at scale.

Electronic Business and Electronic Commerce

Electronic or E–Business involves carrying out your entire business on the Internet or using information technology equipment (i.e. telephone, fax machine, e-mail, ATM, etc). The Electronic or E-Commerce focuses on the sale aspect of the business online or the Internet.

Hardware / Software

Taking a look at the Computer System, the hardware units are the physical components which you can feel and touch, whereas the software are the various units of Computer Programs which interact with the hardware. Some of the hardware components are the CPU (Central Processing Unit), Monitor, Hard Disk, keyboards, mouse, printers, etc. The Programs are the Operating Systems (e.g. Windows, UNIX, Macintosh, DOS, etc), Application Programs (MS Word, Ms Excel, PowerPoint, Access or Oracle Database Management, etc), Utilities (Back-up Utilities and others, etc), Programming Languages (BASIC, COBOL, Pascal, C, Dbase IV, HTML, PHP, etc).

Chapter Two

Strategies for E-Business:

Strategy is a key component in the development and management of e-business. Strategy is what brings about the differentiation in the running of e-Business. A good strategy is what will bring about success in our e-business initiatives and for that matter our focus will have to be geared towards it.

What is a strategy?

Strategy or the management of strategy is required for the success of your e-business initiative. E-Business like any discipline requires strategic management else it is bound to fail. You can have the best technology in place for your e-business initiative but for the business to be successful; there will be the need to align the business with good principles in strategy management.

Strategy can be defined as follows:

Strategy means different to many people who use the concepts but according to Management Experts, Mintzberg et al. (1998), the following are some definitions on Strategy for consideration.

i. **Strategy** is a combination of the use of creative imagination and applied reason.

ii. **Strategy** can also be defined as any course of action for achieving an organization's purpose.

iii. **Strategy** can be regarded as a unifying idea which links purpose and action.

iv. **Strategy** is a process of translating perceived opportunity into successful outcomes, by means of purposive action sustained over a significant period of time.

v. **Strategy as positioning**: Strategy is seen by this school of thought as a matter of choosing an appropriate industry or sector to be in, finding the best market segments and focusing on the preferred value-adding activities. This requires detailed analysis of the data relating to the industrial situations in which the enterprise has to operate in. Such positioning is consistent with either the classical or the evolutionary approach.

vi. **Strategy as planning**: The strategy as a plan is a detailed scheme for allocating resources to achieve the objectives specified according to a prescribed plan. In the view of this school of thought, specialist staff planners take over the strategy role.

Strategy becomes a highly formalized process, divided into easily decomposable steps, delineated by checklists of necessary actions, and supported by techniques relating to the specification of objectives, the establishment of budgets, the spelling out of programmes and operating plan.

vii. **Strategy as a design**: A good strategy is designed to fit organizational capability with environmental opportunity. It is best summarized by the SWOT (i.e. Strength, Weakness, Opportunity and Threat) analysis approach and has very close links with the case study approach pioneered by the Harvard Business School. The school of thought sees strategy as based on the classical approach. It is the rational product of a senior manager, usually the Chief Executive Officer (i.e. CEO), continuosly and deliberately finding a fit between the internal strengths and weaknesses of an enterprise and the external threats and opportunity it faces.

viii. **Strategist as in entrepreneurship**: The strategy, seen by this school of thought as the leader, usually the founder and CEO, is concerned with closely controlling the enterprise in order to realize his or her vision. The leader is an innovator who often works by intuition or imagination to create something new. This shifts the definition of a strategy from a precise design, plan or position to an imprecise vision or even a broad perspective which has to be realized.

Why Strategy?

Without good strategies for your e-business initiative, you are bound to fail. It all starts with the focus on the customer who without them there will be no business. Your true customers are your end-customers but not necessary those who purchase your products and services; who if they lose interest in your products and service you will be out of business. Strategies will have to be adopted to make it easy for the customer to deal with the organization.

In our today's e-business and also e-commerce, the real secret of success revolves around customers. A successful strategy involves building and sustaining business relationship with customers electronically.

Electronic business is not limited to shopping over the Internet. It is also not confined to supply-chain transactions between large trading partners. Electronic Business, which also involves Electronic Commerce, is doing business electronically – all the aspects of doing business. It involves the entire business process that is from advertising and marketing, sales, manufacturing, distribution, customer service, after – sales support, and replenishment of inventory, thus managing the entire customer and product life cycle.

When we engage in e-business, we are applying today's electronic technologies to streamline our business interactions. The technologies do not include the Internet only, but also the advanced telephone systems, interactive TVs, Smart cards, ATMs and a wide range of emerging technologies. Normally these customer – facing technologies are supported behind the scenes by integrated customer databases, call centres, workflows and other secure transactional systems. These mentioned systems will have to interact seemingly, across geographical boundaries.

Creating a successful e-business strategy will certainly help your business stay on the right course. Not only that, but you will be able to realize the following:

i) Increase customer loyalty, which you will have a positive result in your organization.

ii) Reduce the time for your customer service and thus give some joy to customer.

iii) Increase profitability of your organization which eventually will improve upon the dividend for your shareholders.

iv) Reach your customers in the most cost effective with targeted offers.

v) Reduce your costs per transaction drastically for your organization.

Once you have a good e-business system developed for your organization the benefits are endless.

The following are some organizations that have reaped the benefits of developed e-business initiative in the industry they operate:

1) **Amazon** (Url: www.amazon.com) who distributes different type of books and other systems is enjoying the benefits of its e-business initiative. Amazon is a giant global organization who continues to provide jobs to countless people. The company was launched in mid - 1994 by Bezos, the founder.

Apart from the good e-business initiative of Amazon.com, the company ensures that it makes it easy for the customer to deal with it. The company has grown into a big size due the focus of the customers and other partners like suppliers and authors of the various books. Because the company continues to make it easy for its customers, these customers always come back for repeat business and thus have propelled the company for its growth.

Amazon has a database of the profiles of all their customers and before a customer can have access to the company, there will be the need to log into the database with username and password. Once the customer details are correct, the customer is granted access to the system by greeting the customer with his/her first name. Some suggested titles of books can then be made available to the customer to look at. The author of this book has been a customer to Amazon for some time now and he has his page as: www.amazon.com/author/timothy.asiedu. The relationship existing between Amazon and its customers continue to improve upon the loyalty of the customers, which will help improve the profitability of the company.

The following are some useful e-business initiatives worth considering:

i.   Amazon.com has focused on the customer's total experience in doing business with its company.
ii.   Also Amazon's capture of customers' profile information and giving the customers the opportunity to carry an update as and when required is quite commendable.
iii. The ability of Amazon.com to give customers access to their entire transaction history is also a good initiative.
iv.   Amazon.com gives their customers the opportunity to receive proactive e-mail notifications about recommended titles or authors of books and it is a good e-business initiatives.
v.   The ability of making it easy for suppliers to deal with Amazon.com is also a commendable initiative. Giving the products of suppliers to Amazon.com customers in an effective way is something worth following.

2) **Ecobank Ghana Ltd.** (URL: www.ecobank.com) is doing very well in West Africa with regards to its banking business due to its alignment with e-business. The bank is involved in retail, corporate and investment banking and other financial services in Ghana. The organization was founded in 1990 and has over 1,500 as its current employee size. Ecobank Transnational Incorporated (ETI) is the company's parent's company. The bank has its headquarters in Accra, Ghana.

Ecobank is a Pan African bank and it operates in most of the Anglophone and Francophone countries in West Africa. Ecobank prides itself as the best bank in Africa.

The following are some corporate information of Ecobank Ghana Ltd.

Mission and Vision Statement:

Mission Statement: To partner the financial services industry in promoting, developing and managing.

Vision Statement: To migrate Ghana to an electronic payment society.

Core Values: The core values of the bank are as follows:

i.   Integrity
ii.   Teamwork

iii.   Innovation
iv.   Passion
v.   Dependability

Partners: With regards to partners, the bank relates well with most the financial Organizations and other organization in Ghana to achieve its mission. Some of the partners are Ghana Commercial Bank Ltd (GCB), Zenith Bank, Agricultural Development Bank, ABSA Bank, ARB Apex Bank, AirtelTIGO (Mobile Service), Vodafone Ghana (Vodafone Cash Service), MTN Ghana, Fidelity, Stanbic Bank Ltd, Best Point Savings and Loans, SIC Life, First Allied, etc.

E-Commerce: With good relations with Ghana Inter Payment and Settlement Systems Limited (GhIPSS), a subsidiary of Bank of Ghana – Central Bank, Ecobank Ghana Ltd adopts good measures in e-commerce to bring about successful trading activities in the country. Normally the platform provided by GhIPSS enables businesses, Service Providers, Government agencies, etc to offer their goods and services on the Internet and receive payments from domestic (gh-link) ATM Cards. All transactions are carried out in Ghanaian Cedis.

Gh-link e-commerce has two components which are as follows:

i. The Internet Payment Gateway
ii. The 3D Secure Platform

3) **MTN Ghana Ltd.** (URL: www.mtnghana.com) has a greater market share of the telecommunication industry in Ghana due to good strategy for e-business.

Following MTN Ghana is Vodafone Ghana Ltd (URL: www.vodafone.com.gh) and then AirtelTIGO Ghana Ltd (URL: www.airteltigo.com.gh), a resulting organization after a merger of Airtel Ghana Ltd and Tigo Ghana Ltd. The telecommunication industry is quite competitive and the various organizations try as much as possible to adopt good strategies and innovative methods to stay above the competition.

Talking about e-business strategy for the telecommunication industry brings to mind Vodafone Ghana Ltd, who its proactive advertising of its promotional programs is second to none because the author of this book has been using its service for his phone over a decade. The proactive marketing programs of Vodafone Ghana Ltd for its Internet services continue to chalk successes for the organization in varied ways.

4) **Databank Financial Services Ltd.** (URL: www.databankgroup.com) is doing very well in the financial sector, including investments in West Africa due to its alignment with e-business.

A good website has been developed for the organization and on a daily basis, a lot of Ghanaians and foreigners flock to the site to pick a lot of financial, investment and other useful information for good personal and management decisions.

The organization has been running for over two decades and currently has branches in all key regions of Ghana. Apart from Finance, Investment, Brokerage Services and Fund Management, the organization has also good Leadership and Innovation skills.

Also individuals and organizations also visit the website of Databank for its performance at the Ghana Stock Exchange.

5) **Standard Chartered Bank Ghana Ltd.** (URL: www.sc.com), an international bank is doing well in the banking sector of Ghana due to good strategies in e-Business put in place by the organization.

Standard Chartered Bank Gh. Ltd prides itself as the Ghana No. 1 digital bank in Ghana and thus continues to lead in performance in the banking sector in Ghana. The bank has been around for over two decades and currently has a branch in almost every part of the country. The author of this book continues to use the bank's services in Ghana over a decade now due to its excellent services.

Because of the bank's strong network globally, the bank ATM Card is used in almost every part of the world. Most of the bank's customers use the card whenever they travel abroad. Again the customers of the bank can transfer funds from their local accounts to their partners abroad with ease.

6) **Cisco Systems, Inc** (URL: www.cisco.com) has saved millions per year in Customer Service for some years now and does a greater proportion of its business over the Internet through it web site.

Cisco Systems is a world's leader when it comes to electronic commerce with a greater proportion of sales in revenue coming from its website. The company has focused on building a good community of customers who help one another in solving technical questions on its web site. The ability of the company to improve upon its community of loyal customers help improve upon the profitability of the company.

The customer support community was the first and most successful adopted by Cisco Systems. In improving the e-business of Cisco Systems, the company always asked the needs of its customers through surveys to help improve their website. It should all be about the needs of your customers, if you intend to be successful in your e-business journey. In surveying Cisco customers to find out their needs, they complained about what waste their time and based on that information, Cisco Systems used it to improve upon their website.

Another area which Cisco provided for its customers is the price list of its products, denominated in the currencies of various countries the company does business in. Also Cisco has become successful in building trust for its community of customers – a key point in customer loyalty.

Customers are also encouraged to help configure their purchased products with the Information made available on company's website. Also customers have the opportunity to place their orders at the company's website after which the needed quotation is provided.

7) **ARB Apex Bank** (URL: www.arbapexbank.com) is doing well in the banking industry for Ghana due to good initiative for e-Business. The ARB Apex Bank Limited is a 'mini'- Central bank for the Rural and Community Banks (RCBs) in Ghana. The bank has branches in all the various regions in Ghana. The Rural and Community Banks who are the shareholders of the ARB Apex Bank are located in almost every part of the country. The bank has its headquarters at the 9th Road, Gamel Abdel Nasser Avenue, South Ridge, Accra, Ghana.

Some of the functions of ARB Apex Bank are as follows:

   i.   Keep accounts and maintain primary cash reserves
   ii. Monitor, inspect, supervise and ensure compliance.
   iii. Lends fund
   iv. Handle cheque clearing activities.
   v.   Provide training of staff and Directors.
   vi. Guarantee payment instruments
   vii. Provide audit and inspection services.
   ix. Provide ICT services.
   x.   Provide a deposit insurance scheme to protect deposits of customers.
   xi. Provide Fund Management services.
   xii. Supply cash and receive excess cash.

The Bank has its chairman as Dr. Anthony Aubynn and the Managing Director as Kojo Mattah.

8) **IPMC Ghana Ltd.** (URL: www.ipmcghana.com) seems to be doing very well in the area of ICT due to its adoption of good strategy in the area of electronic business.

The company has been in operation for over two decades now in the area Computer Hardware, Software and training/education in Ghana. The company prides

14

itself as No. One (1) in IT Training in Ghana. Regarding training /education the organization has centres in the entire key regions in Ghana of West Africa.

IPMC Ghana Ltd., an Indian ICT organization which has been in Ghana and West Africa for over decade has developed a good website for its operations and is enjoying the rewards of e-business. Apart from developing a good website, the company does not play with its social responsibility for the community that it serves. The company also makes it easy for its customers to deal with them.

9) **Ernest Chemist Ghana Ltd.** (URL: www.ernestchemists.com) is doing very well in the area of pharmaceutical services and products in West Africa due to its alignment with good e-Business initiatives.

Ernest Chemist Ghana Ltd is a leader when it comes to offering pharmaceutical Services and products in West Africa. The company has been operating in Ghana for over two decades and has many awards to its credit in the area of pharmaceuticals.

Ernest Chemist Ghana Ltd. has developed a good website to help the company improve upon its e-Business initiative. Apart from Ghana that the company started at, the company has extended its operations to other parts of West Africa. The pharmaceutical company does very well when it comes to Social Responsibility for the community that it serves. The company also makes it easy for its customers to deal with it.

10) **Enterprise Insurance Co. Ltd.** (URL: www.enterprisegroup.com.gh) also is making giant strides in the insurance industry in West Africa due to good initiatives adopted in the area of e-Business.

Enterprise Insurance is one of the oldest insurance companies to be listed on the Ghana Stock Exchange. The company has five (5) subsidiaries which are as follows:

i)   Enterprise life
ii)   Enterprise Insurance
iii)   Enterprise Trustees
iv)   Enterprise Properties
v)   Enterprise Funeral Services or Transitions.

The Mission of the company is to provide all who come in contact with us their desired Advantage, because they are the best at what they do.

Enterprise Trustees: Enterprise Trustees is the Group's pension subsidiary. It is licensed by the National Pensions Act, 2008 (Act 766) as a Corporate Trustee to administer Tiers 2 and 3 Pensions Schemes.

The company ranks among the biggest pension administrators in Ghana with a portfolio over 27 Schemes (including Employer sponsored Master Trust and personal Pension Schemes) worth over US$120.0M.

11) **African Continental Free Trade Area** (i.e. AfCFTA): This involves a regional block trade, comprising of all members of the African Union who have signed to the trade agreement. These qualified members of the African Union are involved in a regional block free trade operation on the African continent. The Secretariat is located in Accra, Ghana and its operation of a single market in Africa started on the 1st of January, 2021.

E-Commerce operation which forms the main trading activity of the regional block includes the Consumer, the supplier and the AfCFTA Secretariat has been launched in Accra, Ghana and members of the regional block free trade area have commenced business operations on the continent.

The Free Trade of the Regional Block consists of all the members who have appended their signature to the trade agreement. For member States commencement of trade operations in the regional block, only members who have ratified their trade agreements are qualified to participate.

H.E. Wamkele Keabetswe Mene is the first elected Secretary General of the AfCFTA Secretariat. The Secretary General was sworn in on the 19th March, 2020 for a four year period and is based in the new office in Accra, Ghana. The Secretary General is to lead the Secretariat in daily strategies to support the implementation of the AfCFTA.

Members of the regional block also qualify for free movement in the region and also Enjoy other benefits like Right to Residence and Right of Establishment.

Chapter Three

The Benefits and Success of E-Business:

E–Business involves taking your organization to the Internet and the benefits that will accrue to your business are enormous. The Internet with the ubiquitous World Wide Web (i.e. WWW) is broad with varied capabilities, thus opening your organization to the Internet brings to it a wealth of countless opportunities.

Certainly, the benefit that will accrue to your organization through the Internet is great. If you design and implement your e-business correctly, you will see a lot of improvement in your organization's finances and also the speed in moving your products and services to the market; you will also reach countless new customers.

Finance:

Certainly, the Internet with its world wide web (www) helps to improve upon the customer base which eventually improves upon the profitability of your organization, especially in the case of for-profit business.

Talking about growth in size of organization, mention can be made of Amazon, who the Founder, Jeff Bezos started with just three Sun workstations at his garage in Seattle, US is today a giant organization with huge success.

Organizations know that, taking their business to the Internet will result in a diverse range of customers. The fantastic growth of business which will result after adopting good business practices will continue and thus will result in varied customers with improvement in the profitability of that organization.

Speed:

In the past where organizations are normally off-line in most cases, to run successful business you have to rent a shop, recruit some employees to assist in the business running, then the products of the business will be advertised afterwards. As the manager, you will then have to wait for your customers to come in to your store or wait for their order forms. Today as a result of e-business, the story is different since the time and cost of doing business has reduced drastically and the resulting growth and improvement in profitability is better.

Boundless Location of Store:

When your organization moves online, it will be realized that customers of all sizes from different parts of the world will visit your organization through your website. What is critical is to develop good web pages of the website and will attract the customers.

From our discussion, one of the major benefits of the Internet for e-business is bringing your organization with its products and services to people anywhere in the world. Another advantage of running your business online is, your organization may be small with unattractive premises, once the web-pages of the web-site are developed very well, that un-attractive organization of yours can appear very nice on-line.

Success in E-Business:

On many occasions, CEOs and Presidents of various organizations think that once the business moves online, they will be successful without proper strategy. That is not the case anymore.

Since e-business involves business and technology, it is quite important to understand the technological side of the union along with the technology agents of the existing business. To be successful in e-business, there will be the need to structure your business, the need to change the ways you think about business and the practice of integrating technology into your business.

Improvement in Business Architecture:

Because technology is a key component of e-business, business changes are difficult to manage because of the sheer magnitude of the changes. It is realized that organization value does not depend on tangible assets like products and material, rather it is based on intangible like branding, customer relationships and supplier integration.

Change the way you do Business:

In the world of business, if you want to make customers happy, the following associated in running a business will be considered.

Price:

No one likes to be cheated in the running of business. Business that offers excellent services and products with a reasonable price will do well.

Speed:

In the running of business services, no customer will be happy to be delayed. To stay competitive in your business, the products and services need to be delivered fast and efficiently.

Convenience:

Convenience is all that customers cherish in the running of business. Customers appreciate business with smooth processes and also few steps for the processes.

Personalization:

Customers want a situation where they are treated as individuals. The more options made available to the customers with fewer decisions considered in their cases the better and happier they will be.

As business develops their customers' initiative, consideration will have to be given to how technology will be used to address the needs considered above. In e-business, organization should look at innovative ways which will assist the customers to be happy with them.

Changes in Technology:

Integrating Technology into Your Business:

Your task in developing an e-business system for your organization should not rest with only the IT Management department but the business planners need to be involved since there is the business planning and the modeling aspects too.

The website to be developed should consider the requirements of the customer. What applications need to be integrated into the e-business solutions? Consider Amazon.com anytime the customer logs on to their website; normally the customer is greeted with the first name which eventually helps to cement the loyalty of the customer. Occasionally the customer is asked to review some selected books which is OK. Developing an e-business solution involves the innovation you bring to your solution. Customers know that better technology should result in a better shopping experience.

Chapter Four

Customer, an invaluable stakeholder of the organization.

Customers are certainly the key stakeholder for any organization, whether small or big. Without customers there will be no business. True customers are our end customers, who if not satisfied properly can collapse our business or organization. Customers are not the buyers of the products or services, but rather the end users. Government departments and agents have customers, the citizens and the residents they serve. Non-profit organizations have customers, the people whose needs they serve. The churches have customers, the members whose need they serve.

Your ability to set-up a process between you the producer of a product or services, and the end consumer of that product is quite important in ensuring your continual success on the market(s) you serve. If your actual end customers don't value your product and service, sooner or later you will be out of business.

How to Leverage Customer Information:

It is always appropriate that you use your customer information to improve upon the existing relation you have with them.

You also do not need to disturb your customers with unsolicited e-mails. Do ask them what products and services they would like to know about and how they would like to receive that information.

Over time as you learn more about your customers, you will be able to separate your true customers from the ones who cost you money; but first you need to find out who your customers are and make it easy for them to do business with you. This will help a lot and eventually help to cement customer loyalty and thus increase your profitability.

The Technologies that Businesspeople Engaging in E-commerce should understand:

The following are some key technologies used in e-commerce:

Smart Cards:

Smarts Cards can be thought of as a bank ATM card with the ability to store information and perform transactions. For example, smart cards can store customer profile information. It can also store medical information and other vital personal information. The smart card can also hold cash for you and can act as an electronic wallet allowing you to use for the payment of goods and services. Why do you think it is important to understand the use of smart cards? It is because later the smart cards are going to be independent. The smart card in addition to password, a fingerprint or an eye scan will identify you uniquely for all your computer-based services we normally use. The smart card may not be in a form of card, but may be in a form of ring, watch or any suitable item normally carried on our body which can communicate with computers and telephone.

With regards to the issue of the smart card, who is going to carry out that task upon himself or herself? Normally banks, airlines, government agencies, universities and others are going to be responsible for the issuing of the smarts cards. Different parts of the world will have different players issuing these smarts cards since they are less expensive to support than the credit cards are.

Digital Certificates:

A digital certificate enables two entities to establish each other's identity for electronic commerce transactions. In case someone is not standing in front of you or not able to show a form of identification, how are you able to identify that person he/she claims to be? The only way he/she can be identified will be through Digital Certificate. Businesses also must have that form of identification, especially when funds may have to be collected. Otherwise, an imposter may disguise himself or herself to dupe someone especially over the Internet. Digital Certificates can be stored on smart cards or in computer systems and can certify the authenticity of the person performing the transactions.

JAVA:

In computer programming, a computer program which you can easily code is the Java. Why do you think it is important to care about the hottest programming language like Java? The reasons are as follows:

i. Java programs take less time to code than any programming language
ii. Also, programs written in Java are less error prone.
iii. The Java programs can run on any platform like the cell phones, websites and TVset – top box.

Focus on the Customer:

High quality is a measure of excellence taken from the customer's point of view; although producers may grade their goods in terms of quality, whether the product's view of the grading is upheld or not will depend on customer perception.

Customer focus means that quality is conceptualized in terms of the customer's perceptions. The objective of the organization is to identify the requirements of the customer so that the needs of the customer and the organization are met. The needs of the customer have to be identified the first time, so that it does not lead into complications. The processes involved are as follows:

   i. Research
   ii. Specifications
   iii. Delivery
   iv. Review

Normally when customer needs are identified, planning will have to take place in order to establish what has to be ordered. The specifications and standards are determined so that priorities can be established to ensure the products or service delivered meets the expectation of the customer. At this juncture costs and price play a critical role; normally most customers will pay for what is necessary in order to receive what in their view, is a good quality. Profit will then be generated as customers demand this product or service above others.

A customer is normally defined as anyone who receives a product or service. This approach has been extended further to include internal personnel, who are the employee of the organization. Normally, one department in the organization receives product or service from another department and then passes to the third group.

The concept of the internal customer means that each process is viewed as a product so that evaluation takes place at once by the immediate customer or processor.

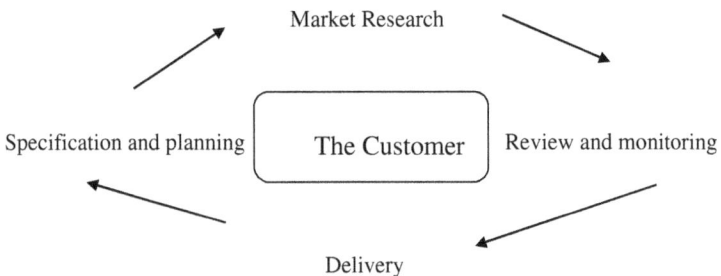

Market Research

Specification and planning   The Customer   Review and monitoring

Delivery

The system will go a long way to eliminate waste and reduce costs, while the overall objective will remain the satisfaction of the external customer. It is expected that the product or service will be expected "right first time "so that the errors will be prevented through the satisfaction of the customer at each stage rather than through a final inspection.

Total Quality Management:

In attempt to focus on the customer's Total Quality Management (TQM), other methods have been put in place in the organization to achieve it. Total Quality Management has other names like Total Quality Improvement (TQI) or Total Quality Control (TQC), or Strategic Quality Management (SQM), or simply as Total Quality. Although these titles seem to be geared towards quality improvement, there are slight differences. Total Quality Management is normally described as a "value-based" approach to quality management. Strategic Quality Management is designed as a practical and pragmatic framework in which the drive towards quality improvement can be sustained while not making claims on Total Quality.

The approach can be recognized, whatever its title, by its objectives. Total (or Strategic) Quality Management can be defined as:

"An Intensive, long – term effort to bring about a change to all the areas of the organization in order to produce the best product and service possible to the needs of the customer ". In some Japanese companies the title Total or Strategic Quality Management is irrelevant. It is simply the way they operate and it does not need a title, although it could be described as "right first time", in order to make sure that it happens. Total quality management can be seen as a metaphor for the process and management of change designed to realign the culture and working practices of an organization for the pursuit of continuous quality improvement.

It can be argued that there have been phases in the evolution of TQM, starting with the idea that processes such as 'quality control', 'quality assurances' and 'statistical quality control' are all aspects of TQM that have to be managed.

In an organization involved with Total Quality Management, quality becomes a standard operating procedure and part of the culture. It is not simply a programme or project, but a way of life. It is normally proved by the quality of materials purchased from suppliers, the approach to defect control on the production line, the appearance of the buildings, the way problems are solved for customers, the way employees are organized in the organization and its communication system. TQM normally depends on the commitment of the customers' interest, requirements and the commitments of everyone to the constant improvement of the quality of everything that the organization does and provides for its customers.

Customer Relation Management:

It is no secret that successful organizations will have happy customers who will be eager to come back and purchase more products from such organizations. In e-business, finding and keeping your customers are a bit different from the normal traditional shops.

To be able to attract and keep customers in an e-business setting, there will be the need to successfully engage in Customer Relationship Management (CRM). What is CRM and what is it involved?

CRM, what is it?

It is normally easy to develop a product or service for people to buy it once. For organization to be successful, it is imperative that a system is developed so that you will have the customers coming back again to buy, normally being referred to as repeat business. CRM is that system which will help the customers to come back again to patronize the products and services. This will imply that everyone in the organization will help to do his/her job well. The following will have to be looked at in developing a good CRM system:

i.   The marketing department will have to create an image of the company so that the customer will love re-visiting the company again.
ii.   The on-line catalog will be easy to use.
iii.   The Re-Order department has to get orders out of the company as fast as possible.
iv.   The Customer Service department should also be able to help solve customer complaints as soon as possible.

To provide the right environment for CRM, the following should be looked at:

i.   Need to Expand Sales: Strategies will have to be adopted to expand sales with the existing customers. How do you also ensure that you identify the needs of the existing clients and then meet them?
ii.   Integrated Information Needs: The existing information of the customers will be helpful in enhancing their stay at the website.
iii.   Use repeated sales processes: The need for smooth customer processes for sales should be adopted to improve sales of products.
iv.   Customer Loyalty: Value will have to be created in the organization, so that the customers become loyal. Some of the strategies will be consistently low price, great customer service and speed in the delivery of service. Whatever strategies are adopted, ensure the customer continue to come back all the time.

Customer Focus:

You must ensure that, you are making it easy for the customer to deal with you. CRM can be complex and its success will depend on how you deliver the best value four your customers, whether the process being adopted is a business – to – business (B2B) one or business – to – customer (B2C) endeavour. Regarding CRM, you will certainly have customers eventually coming back for more business; but how do you ensure the customers are maintained?

Customer Loyalty, a Key to the Profitability of the Organization:

Without your organization customers' loyalty, your business will not be profitable. When your customers are loyal to your organization, the old customers are able to bring on board referrals which eventually help to increase the size of the organization's customers. So it is always appropriate to adopt good strategies to help improve the loyalty of the customers.

In Ghana and other West African countries, most organizations lose a greater proportion of their customers in about five (5) years. How do you ensure that your customers do not defect? Organization who is not able to keep its customers will not be profitable. Electronic Business is able to help build cost effective and loyalty enhancing programs with its profitable customers. New customers are referred to you by your satisfied and loyal customers.

Retention Analysis:

In carrying out retention analysis, it is important we take a look at the individual customers. By studying the buying behaviour of the customers, we will then be able to make out from the pool of customers who and who are helping to make profit and who are not. Once the organizations are able to determine their profitable customers, attention can then be given to the growth of these customers.

In studying the behaviour of the customers, a profit and loss account statement can be prepared on each customer to determine the profitability of that customer. Once these statements are prepared, a determination will then be made of who our profitable customers and who are not.

Evaluating Defected Customers:

Keeping customers do not means lavishing attention on them hoping that your organization will be remembered. Customers stay with your organization because of the value they receive from you.

In most cases it is a bit difficult to make out when losing the customers, customers will defect because of the perceived value of product or services. A product may appear on the market which are innovative or have a better price. The customer immediately sees that option as having a better value and then defect to that organization which provides that product. Certain times, it is a bit difficult to make out that your customers are defecting. If you do not have a system in place in the organization to identify the customers defecting, in most cases it is a bit difficult to see.

In order to put a halt to these defecting of the customers, there will be the need to maintain and actively monitor some key information which are as follows:

i. How many customers have defected?
ii. Those customers who defect, what do they have in common?
iii. Why did the customers defect?

Looking for the Right Customers and Keeping them

So now it is established that the right customers are the profitable customers identified in the profitability analysis. At this stage, it is appropriate we understand the behaviour of these customers. In general, the right customers are those who needs match the value we provide.

Once the behaviour of the right customers have been identified, suitable marketing procedures can then be adopted to attract these customers. In a similar manner, suitable programs can be adopted to avoid attracting these unprofitable customers.

A high level of customer retention means that the organization is delivering a better value than what is offered elsewhere.

Customer Focus will be the Watchword:

In our today's market, organization that are giving attention to measuring customer profitability and have adopted good strategies to retain their customers will have the Strategic Advantage. Organizations who are product focused with little knowledge about the customers, will be struggling to remain profitable.

In our world your ability to identify some of your most profitable customers, and then design suitable e-business solution to cement the relationship will help in your success.

Chapter Five

Are our e-Business Environments secured?

Certainly our world continues to enjoy the benefits of technology, including Internet. Despite the innovation in Technology in our digital environments which promote electronic business, there are some negative elements like cyber-criminals which continue to destabilize our business environments. How do we ensure that there is sanity in our various offices? To develop good strategies to fight against the activities of these cyber-criminals, it is appropriate that good information security measures are adopted to sanitize the digital environment. The following are some Information Security measures which will be adopted during our studies:

1. Securing the Web Server.
2. Information Security Policy
3. Awareness creation, Training and Education
4. Viruses and Anti-Virus Software
5. Good Password Management

Securing the Web Server:

After you have found ways to secure your Local Area Network (LAN), including the server which keeps the application and data of the organization; the next stage will be looking out for ways to secure your web server, or the entities you control to the rest of the world.

The server which has your website and thus connects to the outside world has to be secured properly; otherwise hackers are likely to break into it.

Why Web Server security is needed?

Normally hackers break into organization's web server for the following reasons:

i. Some of these hackers break into the web server in order to change the information posted on the website.
ii. The other reason is that, the hacker can get onto the server to gain access to vital information which in future can be used to gain access to the LAN.

The need to protect your confidential data is quite important in the management of the IT department by the IT Manager and Information Security Manager. If the web server is not protected very well, a hacker can get onto the server and have access to vital information like username and password on the server and later manipulate some applications on the server. This manipulation of the application can later cause the application to malfunction for the employees in the organization who use the application. The intruder also has the ability to steal confidential data or change some of the information on the network, thereby compromising the organization's confidentiality. Again this intruder can also arrange and send this confidential or changed information to customers or other companies, under the impression that it is coming from a legitimate users inside the breached company.

Protecting of the web site:

The web server hosts the website and its protection is key to the integrity of the information which the organization provides. Certain hackers are of the opinion that, once they are able to hack into the organization web server and then manipulate the website, the reputation of that organization will be affected. Some hackers may also have the opinion that, some advertised information may not be correct and as such would like to protest against that information. Whatever may be the reason for the actions of these hackers, it is always very important to protect the integrity of your actual website and ensure that the information you host on your website does not get manipulated. It must be clear that our website will have to be protected against the actions of these hackers; otherwise their actions can drive away certain customers of your organization, since they will feel insecure. The general image of the organization will be affected and eventually the website may have to be re-developed to bring back the reputation of your organization.

The Need to protect your web server:

A plan for web server security can be developed to secure your web server from hackers, preventing access to your LAN and also the manipulation of your website.

It is now clear the problems which occur when our web server is compromised. What are the measures which have to be put in place in order to bring a halt to the actions of these hackers?

Policy:

A clear policy on web security will have to be developed for the organization. In developing the policy on the web security, a clear plan for the use of the server and the web site will have to be worked out.

A policy plan normally helps to identify what is required and what not required on the system. A written policy will also assist others understand what measures are and why they are being enforced. The Internal security measure will not only assist staff from breaking policies, but it will go a long way to identify other possible violations. Again the written policy will also be used as a guide for the people who use the site. This will go a long way to establish trust, which is important to business. A written policy also helps as a warning against policy violations and thus fights against attackers.

The more clearly you can explain your policy and reasons behind it, the easier implementing the system will be for yourself and users. When creating this written policy, there will be the need to be flexible, however some key points outlined below will have to be included:

> ➢ Permissions covering those allowed using the system, when they are allowed to use the system, and what they are allowed to do within the system.
> ➢ The appropriate procedures to follow in adding or removing users' accounts from the system.
> ➢ What the monitoring procedures are and what is done if a security breach is found.
> ➢ What the local and remote login methods are.
> ➢ What is appropriate versus inappropriate behaviour on the system?

Choice of Server:

After developing a good policy, there will be the need to consider the choice of the hardware like the server, switches, routers, firewall, etc. A good choice of hardware with simple features is suitable. It will be appropriate to select suitable systems which will be difficult to break into. After the choice of the hardware server, the software applications will also be considered. Critical software application needed for the running of the web server will have to be considered. The application software not needed for running the web server will have to be disabled. Apart from the server hardware for the web server, there will also be the need to choose the hardware server which will support the LAN and the various software applications. It will be appropriate to choose a software provider who stays up to date with new patches and also have solutions for any new security holes which might be discarded.

Server Location:

The web server is normally the key to the Internet for the organization. That server will provide access to all users of the Internet. It will also serve as link for all Personal computers which access the Internet. The placement of the LAN (with the router) and the web server with reference to the firewall needs to be strategic, in order to escape the activities of the hackers. In your network design the placement of firewall should be such that, users access the firewall before accessing the servers, including the LAN (with the router) in order to check for intruders.

Apart from the firewalls which helps with the security for the servers it will also be appropriate to install security software like Secure on the servers. When installed on say UNIX servers, this Secure software on a continuous basis monitors the activities on the servers like users logging onto the machine and any strange activities. At the close of the day, a report is generated which the IT Manager and Systems Administrator can review.

The Systems Administrator and the IT Manager always needs to be aware on a daily basis about any suspicious activities on the websites and the web server in order to check for early detection of intruders. Another good area to check for activities of intruders is the access of error log files.

Viruses and Anti-Virus Software:

In these days of frequent appearances of Viruses and Spyware on our Computers connected to the Internet, it is advisable to install on your PCs and Servers with the latest version of licensed anti-virus software like McAfee, Norton anti-virus software, Kaspersky anti-virus software, Panda anti-virus software, etc. The Internet is a good breeding ground for the virus and the spyware and on a continuous basis; our PCs and the Servers will have to be scanned to ensure they are secured. Also, on a weekly basis, the engine of the anti-virus software will have to be updated for it to be current.

As part of the policies which need to be developed for the web servers and LAN servers, on a weekly basis the engine of the anti-virus software will have to be updated in order to be current; otherwise new virus will skip through unnoticed whenever the machine is scanned with anti-virus software. New viruses are created on a daily basis by hackers, so the only way they are not escaped during virus check is to have the engine of the anti-virus software updated on a weekly basis.

Apart from the viruses, there are also spyware similar to the virus, which can also attack the PCs and Servers. These spyware can also be cleaned by the anti-virus software. Once these spyware come to your PCs and servers, vital information are leaked on these PCs and Servers to certain sites on the Internet.

Viruses can be destructive and once they are found on your PCs and Servers, some of them can destroy data or program files. Some of these viruses can go to the extent of wiping the entire hard disk of a computer of data and information. Behaviour of a virus normally depends on the type of virus.

Information / Cyber Security Policy:

Since policies are used to define the Security principles, rules and standards to which everyone must conform, the policy document must be given its desired respect and promotion in the digital environment.

The objective of the policy document is as follows:

> ➤ To provide management direction and support for Information / Cyber Security in all the departments and related branches of the organization.
> ➤ To achieve common objectives and direction for Information / Cyber Security management for the entire organization.
> ➤ Also the policy demonstrates management support and commitment for Information / Cyber Security.

The important security document will have to be published and promoted so that it is well – known and respected in the organization. The document will contain the following:

i. Legal and contractual compliance
ii. Security education, awareness and training.
iii. Virus protection, prevention and detection.
iv. Business Continuity Planning.

The policy document must be able to define specific management roles and responsibilities including making reference to an appointed Information Security Manager who must report to the Chief Executive Officer (CEO) and also receive the necessary backing from management. This Senior Manager must have the responsibility of Information / Cyber Security in the organization.

The policy document should also contain all the other policies defined under the Web Server Security. In the policy document must have all responsibilities and accountability of all personnel defined. This should make reference to potential sanctions under employment contracts or prevailing computer misuse legislations where appropriate.

The policy owner is the appointed Information / Cyber Security Manager, who must ensure that there is annual review process defined for the security policy which involves confirming the fitness-for-purpose and making reference of the local information security policy.

The local security policy must be supported by other lower level standards and procedures. The set of standards should form the basis of detailed documentation. The Security policy must also contain the procedure of reporting security incidents in the organization. Also the appointed Information Security must on a weekly basis send Security report to the CEO.

The Local Policy must define:

i.   The overall objectives and scope for information Security for the particular organization.
ii.   The benefits also to be gained in being able to share information with other branches of the organization, external agencies, including customers, suppliers, business partners and authorities.
iii.   The policy document should explicitly be endorsed by the Senior Management of the organization. The policy document should be signed by the CEO of the organization.

Principles of Information Security:

What is involved in Principles of Information Security? The Principles of Information Security are normally general ideas about protecting your organization information. The following are some useful points under Principle of Information Security:

i) Normally there will be the need for laid down procedures which must be implemented and maintained to protect the Confidentiality, Integrity and Availability of your organization information.
ii) It must clearly be understood in the organization that Security deployment is not for a particular person but everyone in the organization must be involved.
iii) The organization processes and systems for the management of Information Security must not be as obstructive as also not necessary to interfere with the conduct of the business.
iv) It is every manager's responsibility to ensure that staff and contractors of your organization know what is expected of them and they act in a secure way to protect the company's information base.
v) Copies of organization 's policy statement must be made available to all employees and Contractors. New employee induction programmes should introduce

and explain the policy document and related standards, procedures and instructions. Instruction guides and rules should be provided for your employees and contractors.

The Role of the Information Asset Security (IAS) Policy:

The following are some questions which should be answered to ensure that local instructions and practices are aligned to business needs and remain relevant.

- Have we been able to identify issues relating to Information Security Instructions to our business?
- Will these security instructions meet our business needs now and in the future?
- How will these instructions be maintained and kept current?
- Are these instructions adequately defined so that they are understood by our customers and Service Providers?
- Can those instructions be translated into specific and measurable Service requirements?

A Sample of an Information Security Policy of ABC & Co. Ltd.

A cover page of the policy document should have something depicting Information and in addition the organization's logo.

The first page of the Security Policy should have the Chief Executive Officer photograph signifying that the organization's management gives full support for Information Security.

Introduction:

The Information Security Policy, which complies with a local company in Ghana, say ABC & Co. Ltd. Security Policy is intended to help users and providers of Information Technology services to understand what they need to know and do to make sure ABC & Co. system stay secure.

Information Security:

Information Security does not concern about the security of computers and the information retained in them only, but it also extends to our documents used in the offices. ABC & Co. Ltd relies fully on its computers and other records which are very vital for its continuation of our business.

There is the need to ensure we set ourselves secured from:

THEFT of computer equipment and that of Computer and documented information which could be useful to our competitors.

DAMAGE to our computer equipment, caused either by accident or intentional.

DISRUPTION to the services of the computer as this will cause temporary loss of access to the information we will need to run the business.

LOSS of the documented information that we need. Documents you can readily locate are as good as lost.

Objectives of the Policy:

This policy:

> ➤ Tells you what Information Security is all about and its importance to the business.
> ➤ Provides and demonstrate management direction and support for Information Security in ABC & Co. Ltd. and its subsidiaries.
> ➤ Tells you who the policy is for and what you need to do.
> ➤ What you need to look out for.
> ➤ This policy will be supported by Information Security standards and procedures.
> ➤ Failure to comply with the policy will not be treated lightly.
> ➤ This particular policy is written for all employee of ABC & Co. Ltd.
> ➤ The policy covers all business information whether on paper, other media, processed by Computer Systems or data network.

It goes further to include ABC PCs, Laptops, mobile phones, scanner, Internet including E-mail, etc.

MAIN QUALITIES OF INFORMATION:

Information Security deals with the three main qualities of information.

CONFIDENTIALITY: The assurance that ABC & Co. Ltd information is not disclosed to unauthorized person within or outside the organization and that the authorized release of information will not cause any loss or business disadvantages.

INTEGRITY: The necessary assurance that information accurately represents the authorized business activities of ABC and is not corrupted or modified by unauthorized persons within or outside organization.

AVAILABILITY: Having firm assurance that information and information systems will be available as and when required for ABC's business needs or for compliance with regulatory or legal disclosure or any other requirement.

GROUND RULES / RESPONSIBILITIES:

1) There is the need to ensure that clear procedures will be implemented and enforced to protect confidentiality, integrity and availability of ABC business information.
2) It will also be the collective effort of every employee to ensure that all company information, particularly the information they are responsible for is secure.
3) Measures to protect information will be based on good risk management practice. This implies that security measures will be strictest over information or equipment whose loss would be most damaging to the business.
4) Open communication should be seen as very critical for success in the business.
5) Managers will have to see to it that business continuity plans and procedures are in place and continually tested. Such strategies are designed to ensure that the business is able to operate even where there has been a security failure to a critical computer or other systems, or a major disaster.
6) Everyone in the organization needs to be aware of Information Security, and must read the Information Security policy and carry out. Users may only use the systems and information they have been authorized to use to do their jobs.

Security Education, Awareness and Training:

All computers users in the organization will be required to undergo Information Security training on their roles and responsibilities under the policy.

Passwords:

The responsibility of passwords rest with the users. Password need to be kept SECRET and managed in a secure way.

> ➢ Password need to be changed regularly.
> ➢ You do not need to write down your Passwords.
> ➢ You do not need also to tell anyone about your passwords.
> ➢ Do not use password that are easy to guess, e.g. Kwame, Daniel, Patrick, etc.

VIRUS Protection, Prevention and Detection

> ➢ Never use any unauthorized software on your organization's Computer System. Also never use a software from a source which cannot be trusted, such as Internet, free disk or games.
> ➢ Before any disk is used on the Computer System, you need to scan the disk for a virus.
> ➢ In a situation where you receive any warning of a virus presence on powering your computer system, shut down your system immediately and contact the Help Desk.

Hardcopy:

All information on paper need to be kept safe. Printout of reports must be collected off the printer after printing. The reports need to be stored in drawers and cabinets. Confidential and sensitive information should be locked away. If any report is not needed it needs to be shredded.

Unattended Terminals:

When you are logged into your computer, it is your duty to ensure that no one uses the systems you are using. You don't need to leave your computer unattended when it is logged on or unprotected.

Copyright:

The ABC Co. Ltd. will only use authorized software. Software covered by copyright, must never be copied without the owner's consent. Any software copied without the owner's consent is illegal and can cause illegal action against you.

Backups:

Information will have to be backed up from our Personal Computers and Servers on a daily basis. The back-ups will then be labelled and later stored in a safe place. The backup will have to be kept away from heat, smoke, food or drink.

Physical Security:

Adequate physical security measures must be taken to protect computer systems and information from theft, damage and misuse.

- ➢ Where possible, use blinds or other screens to stop outsiders from seeing in.
- ➢ It will always be advisable to avoid eating, drinking or smoking near IT Equipment.
- ➢ It is appropriate you lock equipment away, when not in use.
- ➢ There is the need to make sure all portable PCs, mobile phones and other moveable equipment are protected from loss or theft. Those equipment should not be left in hotel rooms, in cars or luggage racks.

Confidential Undertakings:

All employees must sign confidential undertakings, agreeing to safeguard the organization's information and information assets against prejudicial interests or other interests while within employment or anytime afterwards.

- ➢ A security breach occurs when information security measures have failed to work as required for designated situation.
- ➢ A security incident is any circumstances or activity capable of causing or which might have caused the breakdown of the normal course of information flow within ABC & Co. Ltd in contravention of Information Security rules, regulations and responsibilities.
- ➢ All employees of the organization are to ensure that Security Breaches and Incidents are reported quickly to the Information Security Manager or Help Desk and the head of department.

Sample of Information Security:

Examples of Security Incidents and Breaches:

- ➢ Computer viruses
- ➢ Unauthorized removal or "borrowing "of information from company premises.
- ➢ Missing files
- ➢ Information stolen and given to a supplier or a competitor.
- ➢ Theft or loss of equipment
- ➢ Disappearance of sensitive data.
- ➢ Login not working.
- ➢ If the date/time of last login is incorrect.

The local company, ABC & Co. Ltd management is committed to ensuring that the quality of information is outstanding.

In order to ensure that these basic responsibilities are made clearer, the local Information Security Office will produce standards and procedures and other necessary documentation which would help the process and "sell" the organization business.

Policy Review:

In case there any issue which is not clear on Information Security Policy, it should be sent to the Information Security Officer or Manager.

The Policy will be updated on an annual basis. Also, annually a review of the policy document will have to be carried out.

Awareness Creation, Training and Education

Awareness creation, Training and Education in the organization is key for the deployment of Information Security. Once users and technical professionals are clear with issues of Standards, procedures and policies in Information Security, deployment becomes easier. The Information Security Officer / Manager who is the owner will have to organize training / education programmes for the Computer Users and technical professionals so that everyone is clear with what they are supposed to do. Posters and materials on Information Security will have to be posted on notice boards for staff to be clear on issues of Information Security.

Passwords:

Password Management Systems:

The objectives of this section are as follows:

> ➢ To ensure that passwords as the means of user authentication are not compromised
> ➢ To provide an effective interactive facility which ensures quality passwords?

The following are some of the standards and Procedures which must be observed under Password Management Systems:

a. It is required that all Computer Users must have their own unique User IDs and passwords,
b. Also it must be ensured that the password management system must force for a change of the user passwords regularly, say every month or 30 days for classes of users.
c. It shall also be required that there will be no facility for "guest" passwords.

d. Also it will required that the password management system must allow user – initiated passwords change. However excessive rate of change should be regarded as a security exception and thus investigated.

e. Again the password management system must ensure that passwords being changed are not displayed on screen, but that confirmation is performed.

f. Quality checks must be adopted to detect and prevent the use of recognizable strings of characters in passwords. Example: Organization names, Users ids, User names, days, weeks, etc.

g. Systems access must be refused to a User after three unsuccessful log-in attempts, until reset by an authorized System / Security Adminstrator.

h. There must be established procedures for the repair of "forgotten" passwords which do not compromise the accountability of Users.

Chapter Six

IPv6, an invaluable protocol for the e-Business

Protocols are defined as the set of strict rules for the exchange of information. For example when you are involved in a telephone call, there is a protocol in use; otherwise the actual call would be a jumble with both parties talking at once or not at all.

The rules for communication are normally specified by protocols. Protocols are the building units that turn cables and attached computers into smoothly functioning communication systems. Without protocols, network communication would be haphazard and inefficient.

Formally the protocol specification documents a protocol. Protocol specifications describe how to build networks. They detail the order in which computer devices are allowed to communicate on a shared transmission medium, how the devices will check for problems, how large the pieces (i.e. packets) of information sent between nodes will be, the level of resistance the cable medium offer and many other features.

Normally a protocol implementation is one of vendor's implementation of a particular protocol. Network vendors produce their own implementations of protocol specifications. For example, the term "TCP/IP" refers to two specific types of communication protocols (TCP and IP) which are offered by many vendors. The implementation of each is slightly different from all the others.

The protocols which have acquired widespread support over time are called standards. Protocol may become standards as a result of a superior features or simply because they are supported by large, influential vendors.

Every protocol whether standard or not, offers certain features. The physical and Data link layers are often discussed together because they are often implemented together. For example, IEEE 802.3 (the most popular LAN protocol) specifies both the physical and Data Link layers.

IPv6 – Internet Protocol version 6 (IPv6) is the most recent version of the Internet Protocol, the communications protocol that provides an identification and location system for computers on networks and routes traffic across the Internet.

An Internet Protocol version 6 (IPv6) address is a numerical label that is used to identify a network interface of a computer or network node participating in an IPv6 Computer network and for locating it in the network. IP addresses are transmitted in the fields of the packet header to indicate the source and the destination of each network packet. The

IP address of the destination address is used to make decisions about routing IP packets to other networks.

IPv6 is the successor to the first addressing infrastructure of the Internet, Internet Protocol version 4 (IPv4) and is in contrast to IPv4, which is defined with an IP address of a 32 – bit value; IPv6 addresses have a size of 128 bits. Therefore, IPv6 has a vastly enlarged address space compared with IPv4.

IPv6 deployment:

Deployment of Internet Protocol version 6 (IPv6), the next generation of the Internet Protocol, has been in progress since the mid – 2000s. IPv6 was designed as a replacement of IPv4 which has been in use since 1982, and is in the final stages of exhausting its unallocated address space, but still carries most Internet traffic.

Launching of IPv6:

In June 2012, the IPv6 protocol which replaced the IPv4 was launched with a lot of organizations like Google, CISCO, Microsoft Bing, Yahoo, D-Link, AT & T, etc participating in the World IPv6 Launch program. The official website address for the launching of the protocol, IPv6 is www.IPv6.org.

Many Internet Service Providers (ISPs), home networking equipment manufacturers, and web companies around the world united to redefine the global Internet and permanently enabled IPv6 for their products and services on 6th June, 2012. Some of the companies are what have been mentioned above like CISCO, Google, etc. Most of these companies participation in World IPv6 Launch and use of IPv6 around the world has continued to grow.

Join the Launch:

All organizations are welcome to Spread the World and follow along. Internet Service Providers (ISPs) are also encouraged to register as a Participant, if they are enabling IPv6 for their customers.

The Future is forever: World IPv6 Launch Participants:

Thousands of Internet Service Providers (ISP), home networking equipment manufacturers, and web companies around the world have come together to permanently enable the next generation of Internet Protocol (IPv6) for their products and services. While the number of IPv6 – enabled websites, networks, and devices continue to grow, the link above shows the organizations who successfully committed to participating in world IPv6 Launch as of June, 2012.

Visit your RIR's Information sites for IPv6:

AfriNIC's IPv6 project site: https://www.afrinic.net/

APNIC's IPv6 Program: http://www.APNIC.net/community/IPv6

ARIN's IPv6 Program: http://www.arin.net

LACNIC Information centre: http://portalipv6.lacnic.net/en

RIPE NCC's IPv6 Act Now: http://www.ipv6actnow.org

The RIR distributes the Internet Address to various Internet Service Providers in the various countries. The five **RIR** are as follows:

- ➢ **AfriNIC**: AfriNIC is the Internet Registry for Africa and it has the URL: www.afrinic.net. AfriNIC is responsible for the distribution of Internet Address (thus: IPv6) to the various Internet Service Providers (i.e. ISPs) in Africa.

- ➢ **APNIC**: APNIC is the Internet Registry for Asia Pacific region. It has the URL: www.apnic.net. So APNIC is responsible for distributing the IP Address in that region.

- ➢ **ARIN**: ARIN is the Internet Registry for Canada, many Caribbean and the North Atlantic islands, and the United States. It has the URL: www.arin.net. ARIN is responsible for distributing the IP Address in that region.

- ➢ **LACNIC**: LACNIC is the Internet Registry for Latin America and the Carribean. It has the Url: www.lacnic.net. LACNIC is responsible for distributing the Internet Address in that region.

- ➢ **RIPE NCC**: RIPE NIC is the Internet registry for Europe, the Middle East and parts of Central Asia. It has the Url: www.ripe.net. RIPE NCC is responsible for distributing the IP Addresses to the Internet Service Providers in that region.

Contact the Number Resource Organization (NRO):

Website: http://www.nro.net

Global statistics: http://www.nro.net/statistics

Global Policy: http://www.nro.net/policy

Note: The IANA (The Internet Assigned Numbers Authority) distributes the Internet address to the five (5) regional internet registries who intend distribute to the ISPs.
How will customers be affected by the deployment of IPv6 in the network?

Normally end users will not observe any difference in the use of IPv4 or IPv6 address. However, if your organization does not invest in IPv6 infrastructure now, in future your customers will not be able reach your network with their IPv4 address, if the destination is on an IPv6 – only network.

What needs to be done during IPv6 deployment?

i) **Network Operators** should ensure that their networks are IPv6 enabled and can be used by their customers to access other IPv6 networks.
ii) **Hardware vendors** should ensure that their products are IPV6 compliant.
iii) **Software producers** should ensure that their software is IPv6 compliant.
iv) **Content Providers** should prepare networks so that they are accessible using IPv6 as well IPv4.

Note: There is also IPv6 Act Now website with the Url: www.IPv6ActNow.org operated by the RIPE NCC which is a key resource about the deployment of IPv6 and all its stakeholders.

The IPv6 is the next generation of IP addressing, designed to accommodate the future growth of the Internet. The pool of IPv6 addresses contains 340 trillion, trillion, trillion, unique addresses.

How can my staff get IPv6 deployment training?

In case your organization is a member of the RIPE NCC, your staff can attend the RIPE NCC's IPv6 Training Course. The course will normally provide information on where you can get IPv6 addresses and also how you can prepare for your deployment plans. The course is open to all members and the training fee is covered by the membership fees. Information about the RIPE NCC course can be located at the Url: www.ripe.net/traning.

Your staff can attend any of the Commercial IPv6 training centres or can also fall on a consultant who has specialized on IPv6 training.

Associated Organizations:

IAB (Internet Architecture Board) with URL: www.iab.org: The Internet Architecture Board (IAB) is a useful resource for the development of the Internet. The IAB provides a long-range technical direction for Internet development, ensuring the Internet continues to grow and evolve as a platform for global communication and innovation.

The following are the function of the IAB, thus to:

i.   Ensure that the Internet is a trusted medium of communication that provides a solid technical foundation for privacy and security – especially in the light of pervasive surveillance.
ii.   Establish the technical direction for an Internet that will enable billions more people to connect, support the Vision for an Internet of things , and allow mobile networks to flourish, while keeping the core capabilities that have been the foundation of the Internet's success, and
iii. Provide the technical evolution of an open Internet without special controls, especially those which hinder trust in the network.

IANA (Internet Assigned Numbers Authority) with URL: www.iana.org. Another useful resource of the Internet is the IANA. The worldwide coordination of the DNS Root, IP addressing and other Internet protocol resources is carried out by the Internet Assigned Numbers Authority. The functions are as follows:

a) Domain Names
b) Number Resource Coordination of the global IP and AS number spaces, such as allocations made to Regional Internet Registries.
c) Protocol Assignments – The Central repository for protocol name and number registries used in many Internet protocols.

ISOC (Internet Society) with URL: www.isoc.org can be located in almost every country of the world. ISOC has its founding president as Dr. Vinton Cerf. The structure of ISOC is that it has a board of trustee as the head and the under the board is the management team which see to the day to day management of the organization.
ICANN (Internet Corporation for Assigned Names and Numbers) with Url: www.icann.org:
ICANN is a global multistakeholder, private sector organization that manages the Internet resources for the public benefit. ICANN is best known for its technical coordination of the Internet's Domain Name System.

The mission of ICANN is to coordinate the global Internet's system of unique identifiers, in particular to ensure the stable and secure operation of the Internet's unique identifier system.

Specifically the tasks are as follows:

Coordinates the allocation and assignment of the three sets of the unique identifier of the Internet which is as follows:
   a) Domain names (forming a system referred to as DNS)
   b) Internet protocol addresses and autonomous system numbers
   c) Protocol port and parameter number.

Coordinates the operation and evolution of the DNS root name server system,

Coordinates policy development reasonably and appropriately related to technical functions.

ICANN is a not-for –Profit Corporation organized under the California law in 1998, and originally operated under a Memorandum of Understanding with the US Department of Commerce.

NRO (Number Resource Organization) with URL: www.nro.net

Other Protocols:

Apart from the Internet protocols (i.e. IPv6 / IPv4) which have been described exhaustively, there are other protocols like ADSL (mentioned above used by Vodafone Ghana Ltd.), IEEE 802.3 (the most popular LAN protocols), etc.

Application Standards:

TCP/IP has standardised protocols for user service. Examples of such services are ftp (file transfer), smtp (electronic mail) and telnet / rlogin (remote login).

Electronic Mail - SMTP:

The simple Mail Transfer Protocol (SMTP) is the protocol used within TCP / IP for transferring e-mail between hosts.

Chapter Seven

Technology, a Platform to Market your Organization:

Information through Technology is critical for the Success of your organization through e-business. How well information is exchanged is very vital in the success of any business. Information exchange is basically making people aware of the products and services you have. It is the key ingredient of marketing. An organization can have the best products and services and if they are not advertised to customers or marketed, how can the organization's customers know what the organization have? In due course, these products and services will go stale and then become waste; which may collapse the organization.

Types of Information Exchange:

The following are some types of Information exchange, which require consideration:

1. Advertising
2. E-mail and Websites
3. Telemarketing
4. Social Media
5. Networking through colleagues you know.
6. Seminars and trade shows.

Advertising is an effective way to increase awareness of your organization and its products and services. Advertising can be through a newspaper (e.g. Daily Graphic in Ghana, Ghanaian Times, etc), Magazines (e.g. The Africa Report, etc), Brochures, Social Media (Facebook, LinkedIn, Twitter, YouTube, etc), TV and Radio. Depending on the available budget, one can make a suitable choice. It can actually cost less to reach many people through direct mail, social media or seminars because circulation lists are so large. Advertising is a cost effective means of explaining your business to the public. With the suitable design and image selection, you can look like a big organization, even if you are not.

E-mailing is a form of exchange of information by electronic means. Through the World Wide Web (www) of the Internet, or an in-house e-mail system, information can also be exchanged. In a couple of seconds, e-mail messages can be transmitted to colleagues or friends in another country. This form of communication is an economical way of Information exchange. Certainly, the Internet and its world wide web has transformed the society so much. Your products and services could also be advertised on your website, through the Internet.

Telemarketing is also another form of exchange of Information. In this case, the exchange is one through telephone contacts. Unlike the Field Sales Executive, the Telemarketing / Sales Executive does not visit the client but instead sits in his or her office and makes the necessary client contacts on the phone.

Social Media like the Facebook, Twitter, YouTube, LinkedIn and others are also a means for advertising our products and services through Technology. Later in this chapter, a focus will be given to on how we use the Social Media to advertise our products and services.

Networking is also another form of exchange of information through colleagues. You can tell your colleagues by word of mouth of your products and services. This could be done during social gathering. If your products and services are of a quality standard, your colleagues will also pass on the information.

Seminars and trade shows are also a form of exchange of information. Through seminars and trade shows, your products and services could be exhibited to the public. Through this medium, sales could be made of your products and services.

How well you know 4P's in Marketing:

Marketing is the strategy we normally adopt in taking our products and services to the market. Essentially marketing of the products and services consists of 4 main areas.

1. **Product and Service**:

The product or service you bring to the market is key. In looking at your product or service, what to consider are the quality, modernity and simplicity. What will affect your plan for marketing is the demand of the product. It is important to establish the demand or need for your product, so that you can lay the foundation of the marketing plan.

2. **Price**:

Your ability to determine the optimal price (highest price you can charge to sell as much product or service, and be profitable), will depend on the understanding of the market and its competitive environment.

3. **Promotion**:

Promotion involves letting people know what you have to offer and the benefits associated with it. Promotion can further be broken into advertising, special offers, competitions and public relations activities. Advertising can take many forms, from television, using social media to direct mail to a potential customer. What is critical is to ensure that, whatever action is carried out, you need to make sure that the cost to the business is less that the return you will get. The following are some options to consider during advertising:

- Telesales or marketing
- Social Media
- Press release
- Direct mails letters
- Signage
- Flyers
- E-mail

4. **Place**:

The place where you distribute your products, especially when you deal in commodities is quite important. To be able to sell your products efficiently, it must be available in the location (shops or outlet) at the right time (e.g. month-end).

Brand Management:

Brand is linked to the identification of a product and the differentiation from the competitors, through the use of certain name, logo, design or other visual signs.

Brand tends to make the discipline of marketing easier since through branding, the unique identity of an organization is established for the consumer. Through branding, the differences established between two organizations are made clearer.

Brand Loyalty involves trying to achieve a high degree of loyalty and it is very important in the branding process. Loyal consumers are valuable consumers because it is much more difficult to recruit new customers than nursing and keeping existing ones.

Brand Portfolio also represents the range of brands a company has on the market. The ability to manage the brand portfolio relates to strategic issues of brand architecture, market segmentation, and product versus corporate branding.

Brand Equity:

Fundamentally the goal for any brand manager is to endow products and / or services with brand equity.

A Consumer can perceive a brand's equity as the brand value added to the functional product or service by associating it with the brand name.

Brand Strategy:

The aim of the brand strategy is to evaluate the internal and external opportunities of the brand. The brand strategy must be strategic, visioning and proactive rather than tactical and reactive.

The following are some key **Social Media platforms** for consideration:

i.   **Using Facebook to market your products and services**

Facebook (URL: www.facebook.com) helps a lot in marketing of our products and services. The Founder of the global organization is Mark Zuckerberg. Facebook has become so popular that every young person whether involved in selling a product / service or not has an account with the organization. Once you advertise your product through Facebook, the product is likely to be seen by all those connected globally with you through your account. The advertized product or service can be approved by liking and commenting on that product / service.

ii.   **Using LinkedIn to market your products and services**

LinkedIn system (www.linkedin.com) has a database of global professionals. It can serve as a platform to market your products and services to these professionals with varied background. If you need to access credible information about a professional, the right source to turn to is the LinkedIn. Again LinkedIn can help grow your stakeholders like Customers, Suppliers, employee, etc.

iii. **Using Twitter to help with the marketing of your products and services**

Twitter with the URL: www.twitter.com can also be used for advertising. Before the user can Use twitter, it is important to create a twitter account for the individual. Before a User of a twitter can send information to the recipient in a form of tweets, the recipient account needs to be known by the sender or User. Normally the recipient of the tweets has the ability to follow the User of the account. If at a later time, the recipient is no more interested to follow the User or sender, the recipient can un-follow the sender of the tweets which is the User.

iv.   **Using Instagram to help with marketing of your products and services**

The Instagram is a software system which normally helps to develop small to medium business.

v.   **Using YouTube to help with the marketing of your products and services**

The YouTube is a social media which many business professionals turn to for the advertising of their products and services. Before you can use the YouTube, you must have the software and an account created for the individual who intend to carry out the advertising services.

Creating Web Pages for the Website:

The Website has been the standard digital way of organizations to help create the necessary awareness for their products and services. To be able to use the website, there will be the need for the organization to have a domain name say timtechgh.net, Microsoft.com, facebook.com, etc. This domain name creation which is managed globally by ICANN (Internet Corporation for Assigned Names and Numbers) will be used to host the developed website. Normally the domain name is provided locally by an Internet Service Provider (ISP) at a fee. The domain name can have extensions like .com, .net, .edu, .org, .gh, .uk, .de, etc. The website is developed by a software developer through the creation of web pages with contents about the organization, who is the owner. The default web page of the website is normally the index file (i.e. index.html). After the developed website, it is then hosted for say a year by the organization that helped create the domain name for a fee. To maintain a continuity of your website hosting on the Internet yearly, a renewal fee will have to be paid. With your website on the Internet, the organization may not be very big but with good design of the web pages it may appear big.

Chapter Eight

The Internet, an Invaluable Resource:

The Internet helps a lot in e-Business. Because you have more people on-line (on the Internet) than off - line, the Internet is changing the way we do business globally these days. An organization may be small, but its ability to use the Internet efficiently in the form of adopting good website and other good business practices, that small organization can change in size within a year or two through growth. To be successful in your e-business initiatives, you do not only use the Internet but all other electronic tools like the phone, fax, ATM, Hand-held computers, etc

What is the Internet?

The Internet is a network made up of lots of interconnected networks and includes the following:

    i.   World Wide Web (i.e.WWW)
    ii. Electronic Mail (i.e. E-Mail)
    iii. Newsgroups
    iv. FTP

WWW:

The Internet has many services, including the WWW which is graphical in nature. The WWW is the graphical environment that allows text and pictures to be displayed on your computer screen, through a software called Web browsers (e.g. Microsoft Internet explorer, Google Chrome, etc). In addition, sound and movies are also supported on the WWW.

E-mail:

As part of the Internet, there is also the Email which allows users to send and receive messages on a global basis. Through your Internet Service Provider (i.e. ISP), you are able to connect to Internet and send and receive messages at a minimal cost. Whether the recipient of your e-mail is close to you or in a country far away from you, the cost involved in sending the e-mail is about the same and the email message is certain to arrive at its destination.

Certainly, the Electronic Mail has revolutionalized the manner in which we communicate with others, without talking to them. On the Internet, if both the sender and the receiver log on frequently, it is possible to exchange several messages in a day.

The Electronic Mail is an efficient system. E-Mail system saves us a lot of time, since you only read your e-mail message, when you are ready. The e-mail does not interrupt your workday. In a situation, where you are not ready to read your e-mail, or on holidays, your e-mail messages queue in your in-box, till you are ready to read the e-mails at a later time.

The Internet with its abundant resources has software which can provide users with free e-mail systems. You can always have e-mail account created free of charge on the yahoo (URL: www.yahoo.com), google (with URL: www.googlemail.com) and hotmail (URL: www.hotmail.com). In our world today with Wireless Connectivity, you can always access wireless Internet connection when you travel.

E-Mail Account Set-up:

To be able to have an e-mail account, you can always create one through your Internet Service Provider (ISP). Your account can always be your name, initial or nickname. The computer that hosts your e-mail account is called your host Computer. Your account is normally called your **username** and can consist of suitable size of alphabetic characters. In addition to securely use your username for your e-mail services, there will be the need to create password which consist of alphanumeric characters. The password prevents the unauthorized users for logging onto one's computer with the username and gaining access to your email. It is always advisable to choose a password which is difficult to guess by other users, since the characters are not seen when prompted to provide at the time of logging in.

Newsgroup:

Newsgroups are also part of the Internet. They can be accessed through the Web browser and it helps us to take part in discussions of interest to you with likeminded people from around the world. Whatever your interest is, you will be able to find your group to embark in the discussion.

FTP:

FTP (i.e. File Transfer Protocol) is a method by which one can transfer files to and from the Internet. Often this is done using your browser, or you may obtain specialist FTP software programs.

Connecting to the Internet:

To be able to access the Internet, the following will be required:

    i. Desktop Computer or Laptop.
    ii. A modem or router (or access to a Local Area Network, which in turn is connected to the Internet).
    iii. The services of an Internet Service Provider (e.g. Vodafone Ghana Ltd., MTN Ghana Ltd) to provide the connectivity through the signal provision like 4G, 5G, etc.
    iv. A Web browser (such as Internet Explorer or Google Chrome).
    v. Access to Internet search engine.

The author of this book is the Founder of an ICT Organization, TIM Technology Services Ltd (URL: https:// www.timtechgh.net) which started in 2001 in Accra, Ghana. The following are the steps involved in accessing the Internet in his organization:

The Internet Service Provider (ISP) for the organization, TIM Technology Services Ltd is Vodafone Ghana Ltd (URL: http://www.vodafone.com) and the organization subscribes to the monthly broadband Internet services of the ISP. The Internet service by the ISP is an ADSL (Asymmetric Digital Subscriber Line) Wireless broadband service which is made available to the organization through its landline telephone service. What this mean is that, the landline telephone service provides a dual purpose, which is voice and data. Connected to the landline phone is a router which was provided by the ISP upon payment for the organization's registration fee. Once the monthly Internet Service fee is paid by TIM Technology Services Ltd, and the connected wireless router powered, the organization continues to enjoy Internet uninterrupted every month. Since the organization's laptops come with wireless cards, once the laptops are also powered, the Internet signals are received by the laptops. With regards to the desktops, the wireless router is connected to the PCs in the organization through its LAN ports and once the PCs are powered, Internet signals from the ISP are automatically received.

Web Server, what is it?

    - A WWW server is where the information that you browse on the Internet is held.
    - The location of the Web Server may be anywhere in the world.
    - You can use WWW search engines to search for information published on Internet servers.
    - The various servers are connected to the rest of Internet all day.

Data is normally published on the web server which is connected to the Internet and the published data can be read like reading a published book. The WWW server is just a computer not different from the one you have at home but bigger and faster. The WWW server computer must be permanently connected to the Internet so that other people can browse the contents of the server throughout the entire day. Since the cost of a high speed 24hr Internet connection would be too much for people to look at, there are numerous companies who will allow you to rent space on their www servers. Your information can be sent to this rented space and once made available all others can see.

The term web publishing (or hosting) simply means that you have your own WWW server (or space rented on somebody else computer) and you publish data on it. Many individuals use the rented space concepts to host their websites and the bigger organizations will maintain their own separate servers.

Websites and URL:

URLs, the acronym for the Universal Resource Locator are the addresses used to access pages of information on the WWW or the various websites.

Examples are: http://www.microsoft.com, http://www.timtechgh.net and http://www.icann.org.

Understanding the URL:

Considering the URL for TIM Technology Services Ltd, an ICT organization which was started in 2001 in Accra, Ghana. The URL for the organizations is as follows:

http://www.timtechgh.net (i.e. the default filename for the website is index.html).

The Elements of a URL:

An URL has various parts which are worth sharing as follows:

> **Protocol -** Protocols include http, ftp, and news. The most popular protocol is the http, which stands for hypertext transfer protocol? Every web address begins with the http.
> **Server name** The server name is the Internet address of the computer or file server on which the resource resides. Considering TIM Technology Services Ltd website, the server name is www.timtechgh.net.
> **Port number** Port numbers rarely appear in URLs because almost every file server is on the web's default port, which is port 80.
> **Filename**: The filename is normally the name the file has on the server. In case the file is in a folder or sub-folder, the filename should include the path to the file. In a situation where a URL begins with http and does not contain a filename, the default filename (usually index.html) is taken care of.

➢ **Anchor**: The anchor is a named bookmark within an HTML file. Normally the anchors are optional. In a situation where a URL does not contain an anchor, the web browser begins display at the start of the file.

Consider the above case, http://www.timtechgh.net/consulting.html/education.

Protocol: http
Server name: www.timtechgh.net
Filename: Consulting.html
Anchor: education

A website is the data stored on a WWW server and can be freely accessed by people "surfing the Internet ". For instance, Microsoft with its URL indicated above have its own website from which you can download information and software. Before you can see the website of Microsoft, it is very important to know the address of website before it can be used.

In the same manner, if you wish to visit the website of icann, you have to use the URL: http: // www.icann.org.

In view of the fact that, there are many websites of organization on the Internet, you can also use, the search engine to guide you locate some of the website addresses or URLs.

What is a Webmaster?

Underneath most websites, it gives the directions, "to Contact the webmaster, click here". A webmaster, is the person(s) who maintains the website for an organization.

FTP vs HTTP:

In the same way, you can have websites; you can also have FTP sites. The difference between the two is that while website offers a rich mix of text and graphics that can be interpreted by your web browser, FTP sites on the other hand are normally used for storing files that you can download.

HTTP is simply the means by which one can transfer information from a WWW page.

FTP programs: A specialist FTP program can always be obtained to upload or download a lot of files to an FTP sites.

Saving Images on the Internet:

In order to save images the following will have to be observed.

1. Right click on the images that you wish to save to your hard disk. A pop-up menu will be displayed.
2. Click on the <u>Save Picture As</u> command. A Save as dialog box will be displayed allowing you to save the image to disk.

Printing a page from the Internet:

If you wish to print the page that you are viewing then in most browsers you would click on the File drop down menu, and click on the Print.

Beware of Viruses, Use Anti–Virus programs:

Viruses are programs written to cause havoc to the files on our Information System, including the Internet. The Internet is a fertile ground for these viruses and it is always appropriate to install anti-virus programs on your PC to guard against the Information system.

Because new viruses are always emerging, it is important you have a current version of a licensed anti-virus program and once installed on the PC, continuous update of the engine of the anti-virus program will have to be carried out on a weekly basis to bring the software up to date.

Some of the common anti-virus software are the McAfee, Norton, Kaspersky anti-virus software and others.

What is the HTML?

HTML (Hyper Test Mark-up Language) is the code that makes the WWW page work. What happens is that the web pages contain the HTML codes that describe the format of the information with the web page. Normally, when you view a web page, your browser program understands these HTML tags and will format the various pages accordingly. The browser being used will also ensure that you do not see the HTML codes on your computer, only the effects of the codes will be seen.

Organizations making a difference to the Internet:

1. **Internet Society**: Internet Society (i.e. ISOC) with URL: www.isoc.org is a global non-profit organization which helps to shape the growth of the Internet.

Almost every country in the world is represented by ISOC through Chapters. These Chapters in the various countries have their own boards which tend to govern the affairs of the Internet. The Internet Society was founded by Dr. Vinton Cerf, a co-developer of the Internet and also the vice – President of Google, USA. The headquarters of ISOC is in Reston, USA.

Another impactful organization which continues to improve upon the development Internet is the Internet Engineering Task Force (IETF). The IETF is a backbone to the Internet and participants meet often in the year to look at how the Internet can be improved upon technically.

2. **IGF** (i.e. Internet Governance Forum) with Url: www.intgovforum.org seeks to govern the Internet globally. This organization under the administration of Secretary General of the United Nations, converge annually to take stocks of the governance of the Internet. In 2019 the annual meeting took place in Berlin, Germany while last year the global meeting took place online. This year the global annual meeting will take place at Katowice in Poland. The IGF has organizations and individuals as members. Every year themes on Internet Governance are selected which members of the IGF deliberate on.

3. **ICANN** – Internet Corporation for Assigned Names and Numbers with URL: www.icann.org. Refer Chapter six (6) for full information on the organization.

4. **IANA** (Internet Assigned Numbers Authority) with URL: www.iana.org, a global organization helps to distribute IP Addresses to the five (5) global registries, which in turn distribute the IP Addresses to the ISPs in the various countries.

5. **IAB** – Internet Architecture Board with URL: www.iab.org continues to help the Internet grow and evolve as a platform for global communication and innovation. Refer for full function from the chapter six of this book.

6. **Microsoft Inc**, a giant software organization with the founder as Bill Gates has the URL: www.microsoft.com. For over two decade Microsoft continue to make an impact in the software industry in the world. The organization manufactured the popular Windows operating system, the browser, Internet Explorer and the Microsoft office software. The giant company is headquartered in the USA.

7. **IEEE** (i.e. Institute of Electrical and Electronics Engineers) with URL: www.ieee.org is the largest organization in Information, Communication Technology in the world. The author of this book has been a member of the Computer and Communication Societies of IEEE for over a decade. It has its headquarters in the USA. It is a global organization with chapters in almost every country.

8. **Ghana dot com Ltd.**

Ghana Dot Com Ltd is a Ghanaian organization located in Accra and offers varied Internet solution services. The Chairman of the organization also founded the Internet Society in Ghana. He is also the board chairman of Internet Society. The organization has its URL as www.ghana.com. The founder of the organization in the person of Dr. Nii Narku Quaynor received the John Postel award in 2007 and at the early part of the year, was inducted into the Hall of Fame of Internet Society.

9. **MTN Ghana Ltd** (URL: www.mtn.com) is a telecommunication organization making an impact in the area of Internet in Ghana and other West African countries. The organization seems to have the largest market in Ghana, ahead of Vodafone (URL: www.vodafone.com) and Tigo and Airtel Ltd. (URL: www.airteltigo.com).

Searching the Internet:

The Internet can be helpful in the search for Information. The key to unleashing the research potential of the Internet is to know how to use the search engines.

Apart from the normal search engines to conduct a search, you will also learn about human search services that use human being to conduct the search for a fee. Contacting someone for assistance is when it has been a bit difficult for you searching for the information.
The following are some commonly used search engines:

i. Excite
ii. HotBot
iii. Lycos
iv. Webcrawler
v. Yahoo

Search Engine	URL
Excite	http://www.excite.com
G.O.D., a UK Search Engine	http://www.god.co.uk
HotBot	http://www.hotbot.com
Lycos	http://www.lycos.com

UK Plus	http://www.ukplus.co.uk
Web Crawler	http://www.webcrawler.com
Yahoo	http://www.yahoo.com
Yell – UK Yellow Page	http://www.yell.co.uk

Downloading from the Internet:

Downloading files from the Internet can involve text, image, audio & video, and others.

Downloading Text from the Internet:

The quickest way to download text from the Internet is to copy the text unto your windows clipboard, from which you can paste the test into any other windows on your screen.
In downloading a file, it will be required that you use the web browser like Microsoft Internet Explorer, Google Chrome or any suitable one.

Downloading Image from the Internet:

The quickest way to download an image from the Internet is to use your web browser option for saving the image to a file. Once you save the image to a file, you have the option of changing the name of the file. In changing the name of the file, it will be advisable to maintain the extension of the file in the original file.

Internet Etiquettes:

Internet Etiquettes, sometimes called Netiquettes is concerned with the observance of certain rules and conventions that have evolved over time in order to keep the Internet from becoming a free – for – all in which tons of unwanted messages and junk mail would clog your in-box and make the Information Superhighway an unfriendly place to be.

The chapter is concerned with the rules for commercial versus educational use of the Internet, suggest a way for you to become good citizen of the Net (Network citizens are called Netizens). It also defines everyday terms and jargon used on the Internet. Furthermore, Internet Etiquettes refers to the ethics for responsible use of the Internet.

SPAM: The term <u>spam</u> refers to unwanted messages posted to newsgroups or send to a list of users through e-mail. It can be used as a verb or noun. To spam means to send unwanted messages to a list of users on the Internet. Chain letters are spam. Don't send them or forward them.

LURKING: To lurk means to participate in a conversation on the Internet without responding to any of the messages. You receive and read the messages, but you don't say anything in return. Thus, you are lurking. It is ethical to lurk.

FLAMES: On the Internet, Flames is the message written in anger. It can be used as a verb or noun. To flame someone is to send them an angry message. Angry message that people send to you are known as flames.

FIREFIGHTERS: Sometimes flames can get serious, especially when it occurs in a newsgroup or listserv with a lot of users. People will then start sending more heated messages, and things can get so bad. In such a situation, someone will be required to step in to write a message which will restore peace. Since the message put an end to the flames, such peacemakers on the Internet are normally known as firefighters.

SHOUTING: Messages written on the Internet are normally written in lower cases, with capital letters appearing only at the start of the first word of each sentence, and on proper nouns, such as Internet. WHEN YOU WRITE IN ALL CAPS ON THE OTHER HAND, YOU ARE SHOUTING. Shouting involves putting an emphasis by writing in all capital letters. In general you should not shout on the Internet.

Selected Bibliography:

1. DHL Communication Workshop Training Education and Other materials – 1995, by DHL Systems Ltd.
2. Novel, Inc Novell Education – Introduction to Networking – USA, 1993
3. eBusiness – The Beginners Guide by Robert C. Elsenpeter and Toby J. Velte
4. Customer.com, Crown Business, New York, USA, 1998 by Patricia B. Seybold
5. The Sophisticated Marketer by LinkedIn
6. The ABC of Information Security – Part One (1) and Two (2) by Timothy Asiedu.
7. Tim Hannagen –Management Concepts and Practice, Pearson, Prentice Hall,2005
8. Strategies for e-Business success by Erik Brynjolfsson, Glen L. Urban
9. Strategic Management by Colin White
10. Brand Management – Research, Theory and Practice by Tilde Heding, Charlotte F. Knudtzek, Mogens Bjerre
11. Internet Literacy, McGraw Hill, USA - 1999 by Fred T. Hofstetter
12. Larry, Downes; Chunka, Mui. Unleashing the Killer App – Digital Strategies for Market Dominance. Harvard Business School Press, Boston, USA, 1998
13. C.R. Kothari. Research Methodology, Methods and Techniques, New Age International Publication, India, 2004

www.ingramcontent.com/pod-product-compliance
Lightning Source LLC
Chambersburg PA
CBHW020315220326
41598CB00017BA/1568

* 9 7 8 6 1 3 8 9 4 8 0 9 4 *